Mind Is the Builder

Your Life Is the Result

Mind Is the Builder
Your Life Is the Result

Powerful Concepts from the Edgar Cayce Philosophy

BY DICK DAILY

ARE
PRESS

**ASSOCIATION FOR
RESEARCH AND
ENLIGHTENMENT**

A.R.E. Press • Virginia Beach • Virginia

A.R.E. Press
215 67th Street
Virginia Beach, VA 23451-2061

Library of Congress Cataloguing-in-Publication Data
Daily, Dick
  Mind is the builder / by Dick Daily.
    p.   cm.
  Includes bibliographical references.
  ISBN 0-87604-480-1
  1. Parapsychology. 2. Cayce, Edgar, 1877-1945. I. Title.
BF1031.D28. 2004
133.8—dc22

                              2004000023

Cover design by Richard Boyle

*Dedicated in memory of
my initial Cayce mentor
Elsie Sechrist*

Contents

Acknowledgments

I am indebted to the many A.R.E. lecturers and authors who researched the Edgar Cayce readings on the various aspects of mental activity long before I decided to conduct my own research of this important and interesting subject. These include Hugh Lynn Cayce, Charles Thomas Cayce, Harmon Bro, Elsie Sechrist, Herb Puryear, Mark Thurston, Henry Reed, and many others.

Introduction

IF I were asked to select a half dozen of the concepts in the Cayce readings that most provide an underpinning for understanding "who we are," "why we are here," and "how soul growth or spiritual development occurs," *Mind* would be in that list. For example, from the perspective of the Cayce readings, this concept provides the necessary framework for answers to questions about physical problems, psychic experiences and abilities, and the whole creative process.

Even with the mind–body research of the last twenty-five years, many of us slip into equating "mind" with "brain." The definition of mind in the readings is so much broader and deeper than brain. This would be like thinking we understand all of math, when we learn 2+2=4. Here are three examples of the richness and depth of the concept of mind as expressed in the readings:

"Soul is comprised of spirit, mind, and will."

The readings built a picture of the pivotal role of mind in our development through defining some key concepts. We can find these concepts used in different ways in various metaphysical sources and theological writing but their use in the readings is internally consistent. The soul, from the perspective of the readings, is the aspect of each of us, as human beings, that survives the death of the physical body and has existed "since the beginning and will exist forever." It is this aspect that returns in different human bodies for the purpose of growth and development in the process called reincarnation. Each soul maintains both an individuality and an aspect of Oneness. The readings describe the soul as having three aspects: spirit, mind, and will. Spirit might be defined as the creative force of the universe—the God Force, the One Force. Mind is defined in the readings as that which creates patterns from this One Force. It is the builder of these patterns or thoughts. Because the readings consider mind as an aspect of the soul, we are certainly talking about much more than the brain cells between our ears. Will is defined in the readings as our choice-making faculty. We each experience that faculty as we exercise this aspect of our soul daily. These three elements—spirit, the One Force; Mind, the creator of patterns or thoughts; and will, our choice-making faculty—are essential elements in the process of soul development.

Consider using the caterpillar as a metaphor for this set of concepts. I suggest the caterpillar because of the amazing transformation that the caterpillar to butterfly represents for most of us and transformation or soul development is our aim in this whole process described in the readings.

The soul or spiritual body is represented by the caterpillar. In the earth plane it exists with two other bodies—a physical body, our flesh and bones, and our mental body, created by our thoughts and sometimes called thought forms in the readings. In this metaphor, the caterpillar would have three parts, a life force, a cocoon-spinning mechanism, and a muscle. The life force would be represented as analogous to the "spirit" aspect of the soul. The cocoon-spinning mechanism would represent the "mind" and the muscle would represent the "will."

Caterpillar

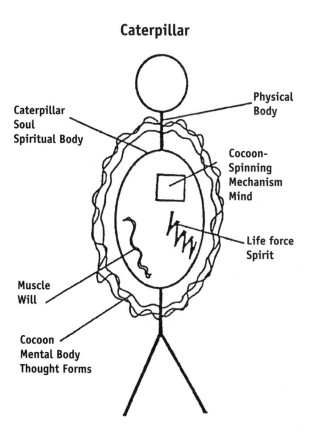

As the mind creates thoughts, these thoughts become patterns and might be thought of as the cocoon spun by the caterpillar. The muscle allows the caterpillar to move. The readings suggest that just as we strengthen a muscle with exercise, we strengthen our will by making choices.

> **"Spirit is the life, mind is the builder, and the physical is the result."**

The term *spirit* is used by us in many different ways. There are the ghosts and spirits of Halloween, the spirit of cooperation, the Christmas spirit, spirits of camphor, spirits that we drink, the Holy Spirit, and so forth. Spirit is used in the readings to refer to the One Force of the universe, or the creative force of the universe—the God Force. The "Mind is the builder" or creator of patterns or thoughts from this One Force. The mind shapes this Energy into forms—or patterns. As these patterns manifest in the physical through our decisions, choices, actions, the physical condition is the result. Energy is patterned by the mind as a thought form in the mental dimension and eventually manifests in the physical or material dimension. Our tendency is to keep our thoughts in a separate compartment from our activities and other aspects of the physical world. More and more, though, I think we see the relationships between the two dimensions, especially in the mind, body, disease, health and healing area, but the readings suggest that this relationship permeates every aspect of life.

"Mind as savior."

The readings suggest that in our attempts to comprehend God, it could be helpful, perhaps especially for those from a Christian background, to consider the Triune concept—Father, Son, Holy Spirit. Because we, as human beings, are in a three-dimensional reality in the earth—physical, mental, spiritual—a helpful parallel can be drawn with the Triune concept of God. Further parallels can be drawn between conscious, subconscious, and superconscious aspects of mind; the five senses, the autonomic nervous system, and the seven spiritual centers or chakras.

Body	Father	Conscious	Five Senses
Mind	Son	Subconscious	Autonomic Nervous System
Spirit	Holy Spirit	Superconscious	Seven Spiritual Centers

The readings even suggest special connections between the body and the five senses, a deeper level of mind and the autonomic nervous system, and the deepest levels of mind, the soul, and the physical body through the seven spiritual centers and their counterparts in the physical body of seven endocrine glands.

" . . . Mind is the Builder. Hence, as each entity finds itself body, mind, soul within itself, it finds the counterpart—Father, Son, Holy Spirit. Thus it is understood how that the mind is the way, even as He has exemplified in the flesh the Way in which each soul may better manifest its relationships to the Creative Force or God, through the *manner* in which each soul, each entity, is treated . . . by itself." 1968-1

" . . . in the experiences in the earth, one only meets self. Learn, then, to stand oft aside and watch self pass by—even in those influences that, at times, are torments to thy mind. Remember, *Mind* is the Builder. Just as Father, Son, Holy Spirit; [you are] body, mind, soul . . . the Master—as the mind is the way . . . one becomes aware through application, through administration of the hopes, the desires, the faith of the soul itself. For, mind is of body and of soul, and when purified in the Christ Consciousness it lives on and on as such." 3292-1

" . . . as we have the Father, the Son, the Holy Spirit, we have—in the awareness in materiality—Body, Mind, Soul. The soul is the real self, the continuous self. The mind is the builder, continuous to the extent that it is constructive, taking hold upon spirituality in such a manner and way as to become constructive . . . that which is constructive and good is continuous . . . " 1620-1

As it is suggested that in a certain way the mind relates to the Son, or the Universal Christ Pattern, and we say that the awareness and manifesting of that pattern is the Way, then within ourselves in a sense, we are saying the mind is the Way. The mind is the savior, so to speak, not that we are separate from God and we move forward or backward by ourselves, but it is only through the mind aspect of our own soul that we are in touch with the mind aspect of the Oneness or God. God works with us especially through the mind aspect of our soul.

We have all heard that we use only a small percentage of our brains in our everyday life. We have also all heard stories of amazing descriptions of "mind over matter"—a desperate mother lifting an overturned car off her child, the role of the mind in healing experiences, the story of Edgar Cayce's psychic ability, and many others. These all suggest that there is a greater potential to be tapped. The Edgar Cayce readings suggest a process, when understood and applied, that has tremendous helpful possibilities for each of us. Dick Daily has done a wonderful job in collecting the references in the Cayce readings to this concept of "Mind is the Builder." It is not light reading that can be skimmed and digested quickly, but when studied, it has tremendous implications.

Charles Thomas Cayce

1

Our Physical, Mental, and Spiritual Bodies

ACCORDING to the Edgar Cayce readings we have not just one body but three bodies. Reading 262-8 says we "are made up of the *physical* body, the *mental* body and the *spiritual* body, each with their attributes and associations and connections that must all work in unison in much the same manner as the organs of the physical body must attune themselves."

In 281-24 we find "There is the physical body . . . the mental body . . . the soul body. They are One, as the Trinity"; and in 341-36 Cayce says, "The mental body and the physical body are as a web or a circle." In 1118-1 we have "in the activities of the physical body there must be the cooperation of the mental body and the soul body; they must coordinate one with another."

In 262-10 Cayce approves as true this statement to be used in the book, *A Search for God:* "Each as an entity is a miniature copy of the universe possessing a physical body, a mental body and a spiritual body. These bodies are so closely associated and related that the vibrations of one affect the other two. The mental especially partakes of the other two; in the physical as the conscious mind and in the spiritual as the superconscious mind." The mental body and the spiritual body detach themselves from the physical body when it expires. The mental body is also known as the astral body, and the spiritual body is also known as the soul body.

In reading 257-22 Cayce relates the mental body with the astral body. In 262-78 he refers to "Mind in relation to the . . . physical, mental and spiritual bodies. Mind in itself . . . is both material and spiritual." In 240-2 we have "the mind is the builder–but remember, the attributes of the mind are a portion of the soul, as *well* as a portion of the material or physical mind."

2

The Conscious, Subconscious, and Superconscious Mind(s)

[THE] conscious mind is [a part] of the material world . . . The subconscious mind may only be fully understood when viewed from the spiritual viewpoint or aspect. The conscious mind rarely gains the entrance to truth in the subconscious, save in rest, sleep, or when such consciousnesses are subjugated through the act of the individual, as in the case of Edgar Cayce . . .
900-59

(Q) Explain and illustrate the difference in the faculties of Mind, Subconscious and Superconscious.
(A) The superconscious mind . . . [is] that of the spiritual entity, and [is] in action only when the subconscious . . . [has] become the conscious mind. The subconscious . . . [is] the superconscious of the *physical* entity, partaking, then, of the soul forces, and of the material plane, as acted

upon through and by [the] mental mind. Hence, the developing in the physical plane [is] through . . . that . . . [which] is given to the soul forces in [the] subconscious mind to live upon.   900-31

(Q) What is the difference in suggestion to the subconscious mind and the conscious mind?

(A) Suggestion to the conscious mind only brings to the mental plane those forces that are of the same character . . . suggestion to the subconscious mind gives its reflection or reaction from the universal . . . or superconscious forces.   3744-1

. . . dreams . . . come to individuals through the subjugation of the conscious mind, and the subconscious being of the soul–when loosed–is able to communicate with the subconscious minds of those whether in the material or the cosmic plane.   243-5

. . . dreams . . . are . . . the correlation of experiences in the subconscious . . . [sleep] as weighed with the body-conscious mind and the experiences of the subconscious entity giving to the conscious mind that of correlated conditions in experience through vision or dream. [These] bring to the entity lessons that, being applied in the life, may bring the better concept of the truths of life . . .   4586-3

. . . there are . . . three elements . . . [which] produce, or . . . cause . . . dreams. In some, we . . . see the interpretations of the subconscious forces attempting to correlate the conscious mind with and about conditions that have been held in the consciousness and are manifestations of this correlation. There are others . . . which are the impressions brought to consciousness through the relation of subconscious forces with and about conditions. Others are the manifestations in an emblematical condition of those conditions of mental [or] physical nature that are to be projected within the mental vision of the individual.   136-4

[In this dream] we have . . . direct communication of the entity in the spirit plane with the entity in the material plane . . . attunement . . . [is] reached when the [conscious mind of the body entity is] subjugated and . . . [in] at-onement with universal forces. This also shows the [body] entity how . . . the entity in the spirit plane . . . is mindful of conditions which transpire . . . in the material plane.   136-48

The information as given or obtained from this body [Edgar Cayce] is gathered from the sources from which the suggestion may derive its information. In this state the conscious mind becomes subjugated to the subconscious, superconscious or soul mind; and may, and does, communicate with like minds, and the subconscious or soul force becomes universal. From any subconscious mind information may be obtained, either from this plane or from the impressions left by the individuals that have gone on before, as we see a mirror reflecting direct that which is before it. It is not the object itself, but that reflected, as in this: The suggestion that reaches through to the subconscious or soul, in this state, gathers information from that as reflected from what has been or is called real or material . . .   3744-3

Edgar Cayce's mind is amenable to suggestion, the same as all other subconscious minds, but in addition . . . it has the power to interpret to the objective mind of others what it acquires from the subconscious mind of other individuals of the same kind. The subconscious mind forgets nothing. The conscious mind receives the impression from without and transfers all thought to the subconscious, where it remains even . . . [after] the conscious [has been] destroyed. The subconscious mind of Edgar Cayce is in direct communication with all other subconscious minds, and is capable of interpreting through his objective mind and imparting impressions received to other objective minds, gathering in this way, all knowledge possessed by millions of other subconscious minds.   294-1

3

Mental Activity During Sleep

IN July of 1932 Edgar Cayce gave a series of three readings in response to a request to explain "just what occurs in the conscious, subconscious and spiritual forces of an entity while in the state known as sleep." These readings say that sleep is a shadow of that state called death. In sleep, as in death, physical consciousness loses its awareness. We are protected during sleep by the "*senses* that are on guard" which are referred to as "the sixth sense" which "partakes of the *accompanying* entity that is ever on guard before the throne of the Creator itself." This accompanying entity "may be trained or submerged or left to its *own* initiative." This entity is also identified as the other self within self.

These readings go on to say "Many words have been used in at-tempting to describe what the spiritual entity of a body is, and what

7

relations this spirit or soul bears with or to the active forces within a physical normal body. Some have chosen to call this the cosmic body, and the cosmic body as a sense in the universal consciousness, or that portion of same that is a part of, or that body with which the individual, or man, is clothed in his advent into the material plane. These are correct in many respects, yet by their very classification, or by calling them by names to designate their faculties or functionings, have been limited in many respects . . . this sixth sense activity, is the activating power or force of the other self. What other self? That which has been builded by the entity or body, or soul, through its experiences as a whole in the material and cosmic world . . . "

[The full text of these readings is included in Appendix B.]

4

Spirit, Mind, and Material Manifestation

THE spiritual is the life, the mental is the builder and the physical or material is the result.   4722–1

What has ever been the builder [of] body, mind and spirit? . . . the expressions are in the physical, the motivative force is the spirit, the mind is the builder.   262–83

[Remember] . . . mental law in mental application; spiritual law in spiritual application . . .

. . . *material* conditions are the *outgrowth* of the application of each; for *mind* [is] the builder; the spirit [is] the creator; [and] the material . . . [is] that created.   900–374

The spiritual is the life, the mental is the builder, the material is the result of that builded through the purposes held by the individual.

622-6

. . . desire is of a threefold nature, and that builded in self finds its response in another; and, as there is the *sincere* desire to build in the mental being of any . . . that will be built; for, life in all its phases is of the threefold nature. *Spirit* is willing: *Mind* is the Builder, the *result* is that *manifested* in the material conditions as surround a body . . . [Your] attitude, then, will be that . . . [which] has been builded . . . [and] has been desired in self as related to another.   5534-1

. . . we are gradually builded to that image created within our own mental being; for, as has been given, the Spirit is the life, the Mind is the active force that, coordinated with the spirit that is of the creative energy, or for God, gives the physical result that is effective in every sense.

270-17

5

Mind Is the Builder

. . . **COME** to the first premise in thinking, in reasoning concerning thinking—Mind is the Builder.   900–239

. . . mind is the builder—whether in spiritual, material or mental, in its fuller term mind is the builder.   2677–1

. . . parental love is necessary—for the mind is the builder, whether in the material, the social, mental or spiritual.   146–2

. . . correlate Spirit, Mind and Materiality. They be one, but the Mind is the Builder—if it is promoted from the source of spiritual truth. 1011–1

. . . Mind is the Builder. Hence the injunction has been to study the spiritual forces, and there will be the ability to see what will be the material results.   3412-2

Mind is the Builder: but unless it be founded in that influence not made by might and power, but by the spirit of truth, of justice, of hope, of patience, of understanding, it may become a stumblingblock to the individual.   1094-1

[Your] brain forces are good. The mental responses to the body are of those natures where there may be builded in the mental . . . those forces, those activities, that become constructive in their nature . . . mind [is] the builder, ever, for physical, mental or spiritual attributes of a body . . .
                                                                        614-1-2

. . . thought, the mind, is the builder. Then, as each soul builds for that it as a soul is to act [accomplish], whether in spirit, in mind or in body, the soul-mind is already in the throes of the influences necessary. Then, when we comprehend we realize there is no time, no space . . . [This means there is no time or space in the dimension of this "soul-mind" activity.]   262-57

. . . life is God, or eternity, and thus is a continuous thing. Various consciousnesses in various spheres of activity are only as a part of the experience, as the mind is the controlling and the building force in the physical being. For, Mind is the Builder. That which is of the spirit is that which is proposed, while that in the physical is as the result of material application.   2772-1

. . . often others—that are less sturdy, less well-set in their ideals as to principle or as to activity—consider the actions of the entity as being questionable and as standing in the light of self's best interests. These are of the mental equipment, yet the *mind* is the builder of the activities, even in the material environs.   441–1

. . . this information may [enable] . . . the entity . . . to better interpret the urges that arise in the mental self. For, the body and the soul is hinged upon the mental . . . in a three–dimensional world: Mind is the Builder and represents that which is [in] the experience of most entities, the Son in the Godhead . . .   2850–1

[Some additional information on Mind as the Builder is included in reading 1947-3. This material may be found in Appendix A.]

6

The Trinity

... **MIND** is the Builder. Hence, as each entity finds itself body, mind, soul within itself, it finds the counterpart—Father, Son, Holy Spirit. Thus it is understood how that the mind is the way, even as He has exemplified in the flesh the Way in which each soul may better manifest its relationships to the Creative Force or God, through the *manner* in which each soul, each entity, is treated . . . by itself.   1968-1

All must coordinate. Just as the Godhead—Father, Son, Holy Spirit— so within self, Body, Mind, Soul. Mind is the Builder: Mind is the Way— as the Christ Consciousness. As it is directed then through the influences of the bodily functions it becomes aware of its oneness, and thus is the guardian force made to be at-one with the whole of the purposes and desires, and the will of the individual.   1646-1

We find in Jupiter the universal consciousness. Notice its position, though, in thy awareness. Move it toward the front, rather than toward the end. For, first in spirit, then in mind, then in materialization. For, Mind is the Builder . . . thy body, thy mind, thy soul [in] the three-dimensional experience of an individual . . . becomes comparable with the Father, the Son and the Holy Spirit. The Son is the Mind. He IS the way. So the mind of self is the way.   2787-1

. . . in the experiences in the earth, one only meets self. Learn, then, to stand oft aside and watch self pass by—even in those influences that, at times, are torments to thy mind. Remember, *Mind* is the Builder. Just as Father, Son, Holy Spirit; [you are] body, mind, soul . . . the Master—as the mind is the way . . . one becomes aware through application, through administration of the hopes, the desires, the faith of the soul itself. For, mind is of body and of soul, and when purified in the Christ Consciousness it lives on and on as such.   3292-1

. . . as we have the Father, the Son, the Holy Spirit, we have—in the awareness in materiality—Body, Mind, Soul. The soul is the real self, the continuous self. The mind is the builder, continuous to the extent that it is constructive, taking hold upon spirituality in such a manner and way as to become constructive . . . that which is constructive and good is continuous . . .   1620-1

7

Purpose and Intent

... **IN** the two there is strength, in the union of purpose and intent— for of the purpose and intent is the mind builded, and the mind is the builder.   900-304

... strength for the physical comes by intent, by the purpose of the mind, for the Mind is the Builder in the physical as well as in the spiritual ...   900-234

... while mind is the builder, it is the purpose, the intent with which an individual applies self mentally, that brings ... physical results into materiality and these should be kept coordinate one with another. For ... there must be those meetings of self in material manifestation of the

ideals and purposes of the spiritual and mental aspirations of an individual.   257-252

First: Know what is thy ideal—in material, in mental, in the spiritual;
and know that they all must be one . . . Mind is the Builder, as Christ is
the Way. Then, as thy imports and thy activities take on the giving to
others of that within thine own experience of which ye have become
convinced, ye become closer and closer to fulfilling the purpose for
which each soul enters the material experience.   1552-1

Mind is the Builder. Hence the building in a purposeful manner becomes a manifested activity in any material experience, according to
the spirit with which it is purposed through the will of the entity.
                                                           2462-2

Know thy ideal, and know that the ideal must be spiritual, and that
Mind is the Builder. The import must be from the spiritual purpose, and
the material results are but the sign of what is being done—and not the
end of what is being accomplished by an entity.   3084-1

. . . in getting, get understanding. In purpose, do not aim for the
material alone; for, with the material things only, false hopes may come.
In the spiritual truths let thy purposes and thy understanding be; for
Mind is the Builder, but the *source* must be in spirituality—that makes for
peace, harmony and contentment . . .   1932-1

8

Building Is from Within

. . . **THY** body is indeed the temple of the living God. *There* He has promised to meet thee. Become aware of that indwelling in the holy of holies in thine own temple-self. For, the Mind is the Builder in the spiritual world. It is the way—even as He is the way.   2246-1

Mind is the Builder, and the association, then, is both divine and material. Hence those who become spiritual-minded dwell within the realms of soul forces, while those who are only material-minded become engrossed in material manifestations—and oft lose self in same.
                                                                              1353-1

Ye find thy body, thy mind, thy soul—thy body the temple of the living God—thy mind the connecting and communicating link with the Divine, through which you may ever receive the answer, if ye will but harken. For Mind is the Builder. That a mind can ask a question signifies (as ye are a part of the divine) that the answer is within self. And the true answer can only be *experienced* by self!   2174-2

. . . all building and replenishing for a physical body is from within, and must be constructed by the mind of the entity; for *Mind* is the *Builder* . . . each cell in the atomic force of the body is as a world of its own, and . . . each cell being in perfect unison, may build . . . that necessary to reconstruct the forces of the body in all its needs.   93-1

. . . the entity is oft very much elated over . . . that which is bubbling . . . from within, that which is growing . . . from within. For remember, as ye sow so shall ye reap. And when that [which] thou hast sown in thine mind (for thine Mind is the Builder) has grown to fruitage it brings [back] that thou hast sown; some sixty, some forty, yea some an hundredfold. For a kindness, a gentleness to a fellow person brings more harmony into self than some great deed that may be wellspoken of. For this is soon forgotten, but the fruits of the spirit . . . experienced in thy daily life—become as wells of living water, springing up within thine self to bring that joy, that harmony, that comes from walking oft with Him.   1183-1

9

Balance

[MAGNIFY] those influences that keep a body mentally, physically, spiritually balanced. For the Mind is the Builder . . . [and] it is both material and spiritual.   1457-1

. . . learn the lesson: that physical must be met in the physical, that mental must be met in the mental, and that spiritual is the directing force—but Mind is the Builder.   3083-1

. . . Mind is the Builder . . . if there will be kept a balance—the physical mind *and* the spiritual mind should cooperate [and] coordinate.

1593-1

Remember that the *Mind is* the *Builder*, and must be tempered with justice, mercy, peace, long–suffering, humbleness of heart, *trueness* of purpose and *bigness* of understanding.   2087–3

. . . look upon all phases; for there is the mental, the material and the spiritual, and these are the phases of man's reaction and man's activity. Do not apply the law of the spiritual in material things, nor the material in spiritual things. Remember that the Mind is the Builder, and the spirit giveth life. And as ye use and dwell upon such, be sure thy ideal is in Him.   2062–1

. . . the [entity] should remember this: The body is made up of the physical, the mental, the spiritual. Each have their laws, which work one with another, and the whole is the physical man; yet, do not treat physical conditions wholly through spiritual or mental laws and expect same to respond as one. Neither treat spiritual or mental conditions as material; for, *Mind* is the Builder, and through the mind *application* of the laws pertaining to physical, mental and spiritual, [each] is made *one* with the whole.   4580–1

Individuals can become too zealous or too active without consideration of the physical, mental and spiritual. True, all influences are first spiritual; but the Mind is the Builder and the body is the result. Spiritualizing the body without the mind being wholly spiritualized may bring such results as we find indicated here, so as to raise even the kundaline forces in the body without their giving full expression.   3481–1

Oft the entity has not taken the time to play . . . The true Uranian will go from the sublime to the ridiculous, materially speaking. Do this rather often. The change is helpful mentally; and the Mind is the Builder, both in spiritual and in material things, as well as being that which keeps the balance and a coordination between the two selves.   1688–6

10

Oneness

. . . **MIND** is the Builder, and as it is lifted up so does it awaken thy fellow man, [and] so does thy service and thy activities become more and more of that at-oneness, that atonement, that consciousness of being one with Him.

827-1

MIND is the Builder, and as its currents run—through those forces of the natural expressions through that felt—they build miracles in the experiences of those that keep that oneness of purpose . . . [by] *being* the expression of Creative Forces in the experience and lives of others.

1463-2

. . . remember that in whatever field of experience thou art, *Mind* is the Builder. Then, make thy mind—in thy material, in thy social, in thy mental activity with thy fellow man as one with Creative Forces, or the *spiritual* things! For these, that may become a part of each soul, may find expression most in the dealings of the individual or the self with its fellow man.   1113-1

(Q) . . . [This] problem concerns the factors of soul evolution. Should mind the builder, be described as the last development because it should not unfold until it has a firm foundation of emotional virtues?

(A) This might be answered Yes and No, both. But if it is presented in that there is kept, willfully . . . that desire to be in the at–onement, then it is necessary for that attainment before it recognizes mind as the way. [This seems to me to say that a firm foundation of emotional virtues is essential, but we must also have an overriding desire for oneness with the *One* before mind becomes *the Way*.]   5749-14

. . . in the material expressions, those disturbances that arise at times confuse individuals in their mental and spiritual developments. Know, as has been given, the Mind is the Builder; yet the mind is both material (or physical) and spiritual. Hence the injunctions that have so oft been given, "Let that mind be in you which was in Christ Jesus, who thought it not robbery to make himself equal with God yet one with Him." Hence, the mental self must be at a oneness with *spiritual* forces, without those condemnations that come so oft . . .   585-4

. . . the basis of . . . knowledge must first be considered in the mind (as the builder) as authentic . . . Whether this applies to chemical, mechanical, art, literature . . . mathematical, astrological or what[not]—for these are of the same basic force . . . as given, all emanation is of *one* force . . . apply that already known, and in application there may be an attainment of more applicable knowledge concerning that individual subject . . . All comes under the one same force . . .   345-2

. . . the *Mind* is the Builder. If the purposes, desires and aims of that mind are selfish, then littleness, narrowness, and those things that make for discouragements and disagreements arise. If they are for the expression of the beautiful, the desire for making "the mental experience to become as an expression of the glory and the oneness of the Creative Forces or energies called God, then may the life, the experiences, grow more and more beautiful in all thy activities day by day.   938-1

11

The Soul Becomes What the
Mind Dwells Upon

... **THE** I AM of the individual ... feeds upon that which it receives from conscious thought or body mind. Hence we see how mind becomes the builder. 900-94

... as Mind is the Builder ... that ye dwell upon, that ye cultivate, *that* is the measure of fruit ye bear in thy daily life. 1472-6

... Mind is the Builder. It is spiritual; it is material. Ye control ... [the mind] through that ye build in same through thine dwelling upon, thine feeding upon, in thine mental self, of self-exaltation [OR] of the glorifying of the God in thee through Him that maketh thee as one with Him.
849-11

. . . [do] not let the mind run hither or yon, but let the mind be rather in the constructive way and manner . . . the mind and the body and the soul are the triune [and thus there is] the feeding of the spiritual self in the ways and manners as the physical body is fed—by thought. For the mind is the builder, and as the soul thinketh so it is.   261-27

. . . the moral life, the home, the mental, are the evidences as to the reverence with which the spiritual things are held in the mental forces of an entity. For Mind being the Builder, that upon which the heart is set, is, as he hath given, "Where thy treasure is, there is thy heart also."
                                                                 1401-1

. . . that which the mind of a *soul* . . . dwells upon it becomes; for Mind is the Builder. And if the mind is in attune with the law of the force that brought the soul into being, it becomes spiritualized in its activity. If the mind is dwelling upon or directed in that desire towards the activities of the carnal influences, then it becomes destructive . . .
                                                                 262-63

(Q) To what extent am I permanently influenced by former unhappy experiences?
(A) As these are allowed to become a part of the warp and woof of the thinking. Remember, the Mind is the Builder. They take hold; but if these are lost in Him and His promises, not only the physical disturbances of the neurosis may be eliminated, but the influences of unhappy experiences may become as nothing.   2269-1

. . . though the entity little understands as yet, if there is the intense study of how *Mind* is indeed the Builder, it will see that what is held in the act of mental vision becomes a reality in the material experience. For Mind is the Builder and that which we think upon may become crimes or miracles. For thoughts are things and as their currents run

through the environs of an entity's experience these become barriers or
stepping stones, dependent upon the manner in which these are laid . . .
For, as the mental dwells upon these thoughts, so does it give strength
[and] power to things that do not appear. And thus does indeed there
become that as is so oft given, that faith *is* the evidence of things not
seen.   906-3

12

Think Constructively and Creatively

(Q) ANY other advice?

(A) Keep the mental and spiritual attitudes in constructive ways of thought; for, the Mind is the Builder.   462-13

. . . Mind is the Builder, whether material or spiritual—as the mind is both material and spiritual-minded as it were. For it takes hold upon life and death. Hence keep thy mind in those activities in which constructive influences and forces are ever the guiding light in thy choices.
                                                                                    1510-1

(Q) How may I overcome vibrations that are not in attune with my own?

(A) [By] filling self's mind (Mind the Builder) with those things that create more and more a unison of *creative* thinking. Whether this be . . . applied to material, spiritual, or purely mental and social relations, be sure they are *creative* in their essence.   303-2

As the mind accepts a condition as being *positive*, it *acts* upon that condition, yet when negative forces are continually set before self . . . and the expectancy is . . . to *destroy*, then *negative* forces become the more active. *Necessary*, then, that the body—*any* body—keep . . . constructive building in the mind; for *Mind* is the Builder.   202-4

. . . in the mental and spiritual, know that though man is a mental body, a spiritual body and a physical body—divided for the purposes of understanding—these are *ever* as one, or remain as one. Hence, let the thought of the body (for Mind is the Builder), the purposes of the body, mind *and* physical, ever be motivated by the spirit of truth that is of the constructive nature for the greater numbers.   1046-1

Keep before the mental body that that will ever be *constructive* in its nature; for the *Mind is* the Builder, the spiritual or the ideal is the life. If the ideal is set in material things, these . . . rust, these . . . corrupt. If the ideal is set in heavenly things, in spiritual things, they grow brighter by use, they grow more harmonious by their age and attunement, and build in the material . . . experience of the body, that which is *satisfying*, in that it brings contentment.   912-1

Do not let . . . outside influences control the body. Within is the ability to make for proper replenishing and proper building of the elements within the body, for not only the resuscitating of deficiencies of any nature but for that which may build in whatsoever manner is desired in the body! Remember, the Mind *is* the Builder . . . each element of the atomic forces of the system is dependent upon every other atomic force to do its duty, its portion of the activities of the system. Constantly see self getting better and better and better! Not that this has to become rote, but *know* there is *nothing* that can separate self from creating within self, those proper elements for the replenishing, except self!   911-3

. . . as Mind is the Builder, keep the mind upon constructive influences; knowing that the Creative Force, or God, is mindful of thee—as thou art a part of that universal consciousness. How personal that influence may become in the experience depends upon how well the entity in its personal self consciously applies the fruits of the spirit of truth. These are: first, love; long-suffering, brotherly love and kindness; patience. Against such there is no law, either spiritual, mental or material; but they *are* of the spirit, and thus mentally constructive, bringing peace and harmony within material manifestation.   2386-1

13

Attitudes and Activities

FEAR *not,* and let not doubt assail thee, for, *Will* will build—with the Mind the Builder.   2720-1

In meeting and cultivating attitudes and activities for these experiences, let the mind—the builder—hold fast to that expressed in, *"Lord, Thou art the Way—Thou wilt direct."*   1223-4

Mind is the Builder . . . Mind is that which makes for the Destiny in the experience of all . . . by an active, positive assurance of the Mind's activity being One in Him.   262-80

... Mind is the Builder, and will bring with those things builded—the material manifestations of harmony [and] joy in doing those things that bring contentment for a life ... an experience worth while.   681-1

Keep the mental attitudes for better creative and constructive influence; these, to be sure, materially aid in keeping the better coordination's towards assimilation and eliminations; for, the Mind is the Builder.

1646-3

[It's] true that the impulses may be set so that the body may *expand* in all its activities. For, as the Mind is the Builder ... so does that mind, that body, that soul, expand to meet the needs of same.   564-1

Keep in a constructive attitude mentally, physically. For the Mind is the Builder, as well as those activities created by the environmental influences of the body and the mind. Hence, be not overcome with the doubts and fears, but overcome them with the consciousness that He maketh [ye] not afraid.   1173-9

... find in thy self how and why God, in His wisdom and mercy, has given thee the opportunity—for thyself ... to be a witness for Him, thy God in the earth. Find that, and ye will begin then with the correct attitude. For, that we find in spirit taketh form in mind. Mind becomes the Builder. The physical body is the result.   3359-1

... as to how or from what source information comes; there are always those reactions from the attitude or that expressed or manifested in the mind of an individual. For ... Mind is the Builder, whether from the material desires, the mental attitude, or the spirit inception that gives growth to the ideas expressed, or ... thoughts in the mind of an individual.   349-17

Know that thy own Mind is the Builder. The mental attitude should be such that ye do not ask of others—thy children or anyone—that ye would not, or do not, do thyself! The attitude should be constructive, ever: that is, with the correction to children or with the advice or counsel to . . . another, ask thyself: "What would I do under the same circumstance?"   2455-1

. . . how was the principle set by the Master? "Thou hast read, thou shall do this or that, but I say unto you, it is in mind (for Mind is the Builder)." It is the attitude that counts. For one may lie just as much with a look as with words. One may be just as deceiving with a smile—yes, how was the betrayal?—by a severe look or with a kiss? These are principles, basic principles that may be applied in thy relationships as teachings to others . . .   4038-1

Set not only in mind but on paper what the entity believes. For what the entity promises itself, this entity will fairly well fulfill—unless it becomes slack in those urges as we find that conflict with the mental processes of the entity. For Mind is the Builder. This keep ever before thee—the attitude of mind. If you expect to make a failure who else is going to expect you to succeed? It must be within yourself. For as has been indicated, think not who will come from heaven or who will come from over the seas to tell you, but know it is within thine own heart, thine own conscience.   3409-1

(Q) Any further advice?
(A) Know first that the physical is builded by the mind, as also are the activities of the spiritual. For the spiritual is only manifested through Mind, the Builder. Hence it is the attitude that the body takes towards things. To doubt in self and self's ability is to almost become defeated before one begins. Hence keep constructive thinking. *Know* it can be done, and only *self* is in the way! But let *good*—and *constructive forces be the watchword* ever; and it *can be done!*   1414-1

14

Avoid Negative Thinking

SEE it in thy mind. For, remember the Mind is the Builder. If it is negative, or doubting, how can it build properly? 2153-11

Mind is the Builder. This is ever indicated in the experiences of individuals who hold to or build resentments, or build differences in any way or manner as related to activities or relationships of the body. For these become a barrier, that may make for destructive forces in the physical as well as in the mental and spiritual attitudes. 1603-2

. . . thoughts are things, and Mind is the Builder. But if ye fill thy mind with the cares of the world day by day, ye may not in the moment give the best that is in . . . the Christ-life . . . 281-39

. . . Mind is the Builder and is both spiritual and material. If there is the activity in such directions that the greater stress is laid upon self and self-indulgence, self-aggrandizement, then the entity grows to be more and more material-minded, more and more selfish, more and more in those activities that bring about disturbing forces in the experience . . .   1464-2

. . . Mind is the Builder, and is both spiritual and very carnal. If there is fed . . . to the mental forces, or upheld or pictured or visioned for the mind, that which builds a carnal force that is indeed of the earth-earthy, the expressions become then rather as in the slough of despair, for their fruit are but the smudges of light.   1152-4

. . . when an entity, a body, fills its mind . . . with . . . carnal . . . experience . . . the mental or physical mind becomes *carnally* directed! The mind is the builder ever, whether in the spirit or in the flesh. If one's mind is filled with those things that . . . [are] of the spirit, that one becomes spiritual-minded.   5753-1

In the physical forces we find there are specific conditions that need correcting—yet . . . these will not give to the system that necessary vital force as will bring to the body the best physical condition until the mental forces are such that the Creative Energy does not poison the body—for Mind is the Builder . . . until there can be some conception of the constructive nature in the mental and physical reaction, there is the continual warring between the mental and the spiritual attributes of a physical body, and especially in *this* body . . . The better conditions to be met in the body at the present time would be attained through the study of those precepts . . . found in . . . Unity, or Christian Science . . .
                                                                                      4627-1

A great dissertation might be given as respecting the existent condi-

tions as seen in this body, and the effect the mental forces of the body
have upon same, and of how the variations in that as is environmental
and hereditary activity in the system are controlled by the mental forces;
for *Mind* is the Builder, and—as has been given—*this* body, in itself, may
create hardships by its manner of thinking . . .   1377-3

[In] being good . . . [be] good for something, mentally, spiritually.
Mind is the Builder. Then, if ye would have less strife and more harmony, build same in thy daily relationships. For when ye complain of
the faults of others, do ye not build such barriers that you cannot speak
kindly or gently to those whom ye have felt or do feel have defrauded
or would defraud thee? How spoke the Master? "It is indeed necessary
that offenses come, but woe unto him by whom they come."   412-9

. . . remember, the Mind is the Builder in material things. It is that
association or that connection between the material and the spiritual
forces, or the without and the within, and their coordination within the
physical functioning of the body itself [which] brings that [which] the
individual builds within self. Then think *constructively!* Do not make for
negative forces that create barriers or hardships in any way or manner.
For these must eventually come back to self.   1192-6

Keep the mental attitude in a constructive manner. Know within self
that the physical elements may be builded; that Mind is the Builder;
that the manner in which the spiritual influences and forces may act
upon the system builds that which is held in the deeper mental force.
Keep it, then *constructive!* Do not think negatively.   1074-1

15

Choices

KNOW that thy Mind is the Builder, and it is true, as given in the days of yore, that *today—now*—there is set before thee good and evil, life and death—*choose thou!* For with the will, that is the heritage of each soul, thou choosest that which is to bring, or will and does bring harmony or peace, or destructive forces with their attributes of every nature.

1632–2

... the abilities are there for weal or woe; and only in the choice by self may the course be taken. For remember, *Mind* is the Builder between the things spiritual (from which all emanate) and that which is material (which is the manifestation that mind seeks to bring ever into the experience of all).

1999–1

. . . the entity is continuously meeting its own self and what it has done toward its ideal. And there is constantly the choice before the mental self (for Mind is the Builder) as to what it will do with its opportunities of every nature in its relationships to its ideal in the activities towards others.   1632-3

. . . remember, Mind is the Builder—and creates that influence for the choice *by* the relationships of its activity for constructive forces in the experience; or indulgences that become in the nature of self-indulgence, self-glorification, self-satisfaction.   880-2

It is very true that *Mind* is the control, Mind is the Builder, and Mind may be made wholly a spiritual force or source.   1471-1

Know that it was well given, "The *spirit* is willing, the *flesh* is weak." The *Mind* is the Builder. The conceptions must be either spiritual natures, or of self-indulgences. These are ever set before self. Choose to manifest rather that of the spiritual.   853-1

. . . know that *Mind* is the Builder, also . . . the liberator from confusion, or the force that may prevent peace or harmony; depending upon . . . that ye have chosen within thy inner self as thy ideal.   2410-1

. . . as the Son is the way, so is the Mind the Builder—that makes for both at-onement with Him and a condition of being at variance with Him. He having passed this way makes the way for each soul to find . . . the manner of administering or applying the ideal chosen by self . . . each soul is a free-willed individual, and chooses the way and the application. For it is either the co-worker with God in creation—and creative then in its attitude, in its thought, in its application of tenets and truths day by day; OR in attune with that which is at variance, and thus

besetting or putting stumbling blocks in the way of others along the
way.   2549-1

The development or retardment through such experiences will de-
pend upon the choice the entity makes as to its ideal. Know that Mind
is the Builder: and, if there is the trust in the Creative Forces that find
expression through the mental, as a materialization in the experience,
such adverse influences may be turned more and more into periods,
days, weeks, months and years of success. Do not let such success "go to
the head" and self become important—for it is what ye may *do* and *be* for
others that is important in thy experience!   2301-1

All that is material once existed in spirit, or [in] the soul of the entity.
Mind becomes the Builder, the physical becomes the result. It depends,
then, upon the materials—or the spirit with which one is prompted.
Thus it behooves the entity to analyze self, not merely as an entity but
as to universal laws and universal consciousness. Begin with this, then
as a fact:
    The Lord thy God is one. The self—as an individual entity, body, mind,
soul—is one. The soul is a child of God, or a thought, a corpuscle in the
heart of God. Yet the entity, thine own soul, has been given a will to use
the attributes of soul, mind and body to thine own purposes. Thus as
the individual entity applies self in relationships to those facts, the entity shows itself to be a true child or a wayward child, or a rebellious
child, of the Creative Force or God.   3376-2

    . . . the entity gained, lost and gained; gained when there were those
activities . . . that made for the greater consideration of the groups and
masses; lost when there was the indulgence in the satisfying or gratify-
ing of self's own interests. These may become stumbling blocks in the
entity's experience even in the present. Look to that which is an ideal,
and be sure it is founded in that of spiritual import. For, every fact has
its inception in spirit; Mind is the Builder, the material expression is the

outcome of one of these upon the other. The spirit is of creation, or God; the mind is as of an individual taking hold upon both materiality and spirituality. The choice is in the hands of the individual, Use thy talents well.   2786-1

16

Ideals

WHAT is thy ideal mentally? Know that in the material, Mind is the Builder. Are thy ideals and thy conversations with thy associates consistent? They should be.   2524–5

Mind is the Builder, and that entertained, that builded, that pattern set in same, is that to which the body, the mind and the soul attains by this constancy held before same.   370–3

Know that Mind is the Builder. That which is conceived in the spirit is materialized through the mental processes, according to what is done with ideas and ideals. Thus ye build to understanding . . .   2791–1

Mind is the Builder. The mind uses its spiritual ideals to build upon
. . . it is the interference by the material desires that prevents a body and
a mind from keeping in perfect accord with its ideal.   357-13

. . . conclusions, even from the opinions of others . . . [are] very well,
if the ideals of the entity are ideals and not ideas alone. Ideals have their
basic principle in spiritual import. While the Mind is the Builder, that as
bespeaks of self or selfishness is ideas, not ideals.   2716-1

. . . each individual should first analyze itself as to what its beliefs,
tenets and ideas are, as to material, moral and—most of all—spiritual
ideals. Then . . . [know] that Mind is the Builder. Unless the tenets of the
mind are of [a] spiritual nature and spiritual construction . . . the building may not be proper . . .   520-3

. . . set thyself to be the control, through thy mental self (for Mind is
the Builder), and budget thy time—for physical development, physical
relaxation, physical improvement, mental relaxation, mental taxation,
mental improvement and mental development. And let the basic forces
ever be prompted by thy spiritual ideals.   1206-13

Know . . . in whom ye believe and in what ye believe, spiritually;
then know what is thy idea and also thy ideal mentally. For Mind is the
Builder. For it partakes both of materiality and eternity and spirituality.
These know for these are true. The results in thy experience materially
should be, will be, when ye are assured, pleasing first in the sight of
God and harmonious in thine own experience.   3481-2

Know that all that comes into materialization or into physical being
is first patterned in mind and in spirit. Mind is the Builder, and your
purpose is dependent upon the spirit or what mortar, what water—

(those things that go to make materiality active in the earth)—you use, as to what is the character of the body, mind or structure that ye, as an entity, create.   3541-1

. . . first there must be set in self that which is the basis for its ideal; not as in flesh, not as in attainment, not as in position, power, fame [or] fortune; but the ideal in the spiritual sense. For the Mind is the Builder. And ye are coming into that bright light, [the] white light of thine experience in thine loving service to thy fellow man, that has made, [and] is making for the advancements in thine own material self, in thine own mental self; and [also] a growth in thine own soul-understanding.

846-2

. . . the ideals must be one, and their spiritual concepts, spiritual aspirations, spiritual hopes, spiritual desires shall be the pattern for each phase of the entity's experience in the material world—in the mental world, in the spiritual world. And know that Mind is the Builder. Oft things said under the breath and never given expression to, in word, may be as potent as though you railed for a period. For, ye are measured with that measurement in body, in mind, in spirit, that ye mete to others.   2751-1

First, in self find what are the promptings for thy activities, in relationships to thy fellow man. Know thy ideal; not of mental or material import but of the spiritual. For *Mind* is the Builder, the Spirit is the motivative force and is the turning of self to the things of the spirit . . . may the promptings make for that in the experience, in whatever direction the activities may be taken, to be of a *constructive* nature . . . only these bring peace, harmony, joy of life, of service, of activity.   892-1

Mind is the Builder, being both the spiritual and material; and the consciousness of same reaches man only in his awareness of his consciousness through the senses of his physical being . . . the senses take on an activity in which they may be directed in that awareness, that consciousness of the spiritual self as well as in the physical indulgences or appetites or activities that become as a portion of the selfish nature of the . . . entity. It behooves the entity first . . . then to know, to conceive, to imagine, to become aware of that which is its ideal.   826-11

There is that same element in the mental body—as in the physical—to be kept fit. That is, do not expect to have a mental derangement in the image being created for recuperative forces for the body and expect a perfect physical body; for the Mind is the Builder, and that as is set as a pattern before the mental forces adds to those portions of the system in their respective units of force created in the body, mentally, physically, spiritually. Then, to coordinate all these, keep mind aright. Keep the physical aright. Let the mental being [be] keep aright, for these—as given—physically—are set. The mental may be warped—the mental may be turned aside. Do not ask "What is right?" Present thine body the living sacrifice, holy and acceptable unto Him, which is but a reasonable service—for, as has been seen and understood by this body–mind, those conditions arising in a physical being come from that of a misdirected energy of a unit of the whole physical body. The physical being, then, subject to the mental. The mental, being related to the spiritual, needs that full cooperation that is necessary for a well–rounded life; [so] that [these] may be used to reflect that gained in this mundane sphere. Apply self! Keep body and mind attuned to that oneness of purpose as is set in Him . . .   2675-8

17

Application

THESE dreams . . . are lessons to be applied . . . and are the correlating of the developments of the mind, the body, the soul forces of same, acted upon by the soul forces of [the] subconscious mind . . . and emblematically given to the mind as instructions . . .   294-36

. . . [dreams] are for the entity's edification. Will they be applied in the physical or material life? For, the dreams and visions are as experiences to the mental forces, and the mental or mind is the Builder.

137-92

(Q) What specific things can I do to further my spiritual . . . and mental development?

(A) . . . require of self—specifically—that there be the *material* demonstrations of the spiritual thoughts in relationships to others . . . studying these [demonstrations] will bring mental and spiritual development. The Mind is the Builder. If it [the Mind] is founded in spirit and in truth, there may come the knowledge of practical application.   476-1

. . . knowing of those conditions as are presented, through that same house in which the Father's mansions are builded, is only an application of those powers supplied through that same force . . . or, as may be applied in that of the mental ability in man as the gift of the creative force. *Man* has a creative force from the divine . . . Man may *mis*-apply . . . [his] own creative force . . . [and] become a destruction to self. Man's applying that force . . . [as] directed gives light, life and abundance, in every way and manner. *Mind*, the Builder.   900-227

. . . the Mind is the Builder, [and] the activities of the conscious man [powers and] gives results . . . Remember, "Large oaks from small acorns grow." Remember the grain of sand is the foundation of the seashore. Remember that it was the still small voice, and not the wind nor the lightning that was the voice of the Creative Energy that rules the world. Remember, then, that action—with the correct purpose—builds in the hearts and minds of individuals who are co-workers and ambassadors of that living force we call God.   3976-5

. . . as thoughts take hold, and as Mind is the Builder, these become then the storehouses of knowledge . . . [and] power, which if applied in a *constructive* manner brings harmony. But if it is applied in . . . selfishness, in aggrandizements, in pleasure, it may only bring the husks of desire that may not be satisfied. These the entity has learned and is learning. And the more these are applied, the greater may be the peace and harmony that is being sought by the entity in its associations with its fellow man.   1613-4

He has given thee a mind, a body, an earth, and land in which to dwell. He has set the sun, the moon, the planets, the stars about thee to remind thee, even as the psalmist gave, "Day unto day uttereth speech, night unto night sheweth knowledge." These ye know, these ye have comprehended; but, do ye take thought of same? *Know* that . . . thy *Mind*—is the Builder! As what does thy soul appear? A spot, a blot upon the sun? or as that which giveth light unto those who sit in darkness, to those who cry aloud for hope? Hast thou created hope in thy association with thy fellow men?   5757-1

Mind is the Builder . . . [and] it is both spiritual and material, according to its application in the associations with conditions, individuals or circumstances.   1158-12

. . . Mind, the Builder, may bring crimes or miracles into the experience of self as well as others—dependent upon the application of same in the experience.   1908-1

The Mind is the Builder, for the holding of a problem does not change it one whit—it is what one does about it that makes the change! Then to know to do good and not to do it is sin.   1747-5

. . . [The] entity may attain. And how? By applying self in that thou knowest to do, as to the spiritual things in the inner self. For, the mind is the builder; whether it has its inception from the spiritual forces or the carnal forces.   553-1

. . . Mind is the Builder . . . building is how each applies . . . every thought is . . . a deed. In . . . words and in the application of same man builds . . . [the] character and manifestation of that which man worships . . . the worshipful mind is the builder.   996-11

Ye have taught, ye have preached it in thy literature and thy activities, as to how and as to what spirituality, practically applied in the life of the individual, should create for its environs, if the mental and body-mind is the Builder of the body. Why not try practicing it in self?

3395-1

As the entity, an individual, then applies, it becomes aware—through patience, through time, through space—of its relationship to the Godhead—Father, Son, Holy Spirit. In self it finds body, mind, soul. As the Son is the builder, so the Mind is the Builder in the individual.

3508-1

. . . if ye would have life, ye must give it! As the laws are in the spiritual, so in the mental. For the Mind *is* the Builder . . . If ye would have love, ye must show thyself lovely. If ye would have friends, ye must show thyself friendly. If ye would have peace and harmony, forget self and make for harmony and peace in thy associations.   1650-1

The Mind is the Builder. And this entity is especially endowed with, and has developed through the experiences in the earth plane, an un-usual ability to analyze those problems of most any nature. Spiritualiz-ing the abilities here, there is little that may not be accomplished, that the entity puts its mind to . . .   2851-1

. . . dreams . . . are as lessons, either directly or emblematically, and the body consciousness experiences in same those lessons that— applied in the physical forces—become a portion of the inner con-science; for, Mind the Builder—being conscious, subconscious [and] superconscious . . . each . . . [is a] phase of the whole . . . Applying same . . . one builds to that attained through the ability to apply the lessons and the truths gained by experiences in and through earth's phases of life.   900-338

SEEKING INFORMATION ON

holistic health, spirituality, dreams, intuition or ancient civilizations?
Call 1-800-723-1112, visit our Web site, or mail in this postage-paid card for a FREE catalog of books and membership information.

Name: _____

Address: _____

City: _____

State/Province: _____

Postal/Zip Code: _____ Country: _____

Association for Research and Enlightenment, Inc.
215 67th Street
Virginia Beach, VA 23451-2061

For faster service, call 1-800-723-1112.
www.edgarcayce.org

PBIN

BUSINESS REPLY MAIL

FIRST CLASS   PERMIT NO. 2456   VIRGINIA BEACH, VA

POSTAGE WILL BE PAID BY ADDRESSEE

**ASSOCIATION FOR RESEARCH
AND ENLIGHTENMENT INC
215 67TH STREET
VIRGINIA BEACH VA 23451-9819**

The entity finds itself in a three-dimensional world—body, mind, soul—just as in the earth the three-dimensional concept of the Godhead is the Father, the Son and the Holy Spirit. The body–mind is the builder. Mind is ever the Builder. For in the beginning God moved and mind, knowledge, came into being—and the earth and the fullness thereof became the result of same. So the entity finds in self those latent talents or abilities. Know deep within self that it is true, you'd better be doing something, even if it's wrong . . . [than] doing nothing at all. For the Mind is the Builder, but in self.   5000-1

. . . force as is being picturalized and brought to the attention of others may . . . give the more perfect understanding of how Mind, the builder; Mind the destructive force; Mind, the actor . . . is related to that . . . *force manifested* . . . in the material world. For, through each is seen . . . the action of Mind, whether of that pertaining to conditions for the body, in the diet, in the manner of social etiquette, in the manner of that that brings the monies to be used in any force or manner. Then take all, build on all, using all, in the way that brings the better under-standing to self and to others.   900-180

. . . the entity is body, mind and soul. The soul is eternal, it is indi-vidual. The Mind is the Builder, and weaves that into the being of the soul that it, the soul–entity, presents to its Creator as the usage of the talents given. The body is merely the channel through which there is material activity. Then as the entity uses its abilities, its faults, its virtues, as an emissary, as a witness for the Creative Forces, so may the entity present to its Maker, its Savior, its Lord, its King, that which the entity has done *about* the opportunity given.   2550-1

18

Growth

... **[KNOW]** that as Mind is the Builder, unless its promptings and its first and basic influence are in the spirit of fairness and justice and mercy to the fellow man, it may not grow in its maturity to a thing of joy or beauty in thy life.   256-5

The entity gained, spiritually, mentally, materially. Know that in the present these are one, and are related one to another, but the *Mind* is the Builder. For it [Mind] is that invisible connection between the spiritual body and the physical being ...   3032-2

What is sown in spirit may *grow* in mind, may find fruit in materiality—and ... this changed may be just the reverse—that the dwelling

upon material influence of selfish natures separates spirit from the control of Mind, the Builder.   2408-1

. . . as is seen builded . . . sincerity of purpose . . . building to and for
an ideal. Whether as to mental or physical, or spiritual influences, these
are the *building* for the entity. The mental or the Mind, the Builder, guided
by the carnal or by the spirit, makes for that that becomes the miracles
or becomes the hellion.   1717-1

. . . periods arise when those closest in the experiences term the
entity as being rather hardheaded when he shouldn't be. These are as
those changes in the influences that arise. What one does with such
urges makes for its mental and soul development. For Mind is the
Builder, [and] Mind is both material *and* spiritual.   877-1

Keeping the faith that arises from the innate spiritual enfoldment,
use the Mind as the Builder, the Christ as the leader, and ye will come to
the knowledge of those things that keep the body, the mind, in those
attunements in such a manner as to be a joy to all who may become
even acquainted with thee.   3342-1

Mind is the Builder. And as it flows through the physical and the
spiritual self, it takes hold upon that ye cultivate in thy experiences. For
ye grow in grace and knowledge, and in understanding, by cultivating
in thy consciousness the awareness of whether it is thy own indulgences, thy own purposes ye are cultivating, or that purpose the Lord
thy God hath for and with thee.   1470-2

The entity was among those that *ruled* in that period, and counseled
well for the peoples in that land. Gaining for self in the service . . . to
others; feeling, knowing, that . . . service to others . . . lending to the

Creative Energies . . . builds for self that bulwark of understanding that may not be surpassed by any mind: and Mind being the Builder, is able to control, both for the material and spiritual portion of the individual.

2908-1

. . . whatsoever individuals, or souls, sow, or think, or imagine in the mental self, they build into their own lives. Just as the body physically oft becomes subject to, or attuned to, those influences upon which it— the body—subsists, so the Mind—as the Builder in the spiritual relation- ships, or in relationships of the body-physical to the spiritual things grows, or is inclined and acts towards the activities with which it be- comes related day by day.   2081-1

As to the sojourns in the earth—these find expression through the emotions of the body; of a mental nature, yet [are] the growth. The Mind is the Builder, though it is ever tempered with the spiritual im- port. For, life is continuous. Though the entity may have had various names and experiences in the earthly sojourns, it is still the same entity, or spirit and mind. As to the physical expressions—these change. For, all is under the law.   2784-1

. . . *Mind is* the Builder. If the thought is directed in those channels that consider most the material things, then carnal must be the outlook. If the thought is directed in those lines that consider first and foremost that the greater command to men of all ages, places or climes has been that the Great Spirit of Truth is *eminent, is* in the forefront, then the build- ing must be that which is of the sure foundation—that is found in Him.

2126-1

. . . the whole that is a growth . . . are the words of truth, if they are prompted by or from thine inner self toward thy fellow man; not for self but that the glory of the Father through thee may find its expression and growth in [the] material world. For matter is the expression of spirit *moving* in the material world. The Mind is the Builder in which there are all of its phases and manifestations . . . thou hast set before thee a *great* undertaking. Be thou faithful to that which has been entrusted unto thee. From whom? From the Creative Forces . . .   520-4

As ye experience, that ye think, that ye study, that ye dwell upon mentally, ye become . . . more influenced by [these]—in thy mental self and physical self. And ye either feed thy soul upon the husks of right and righteousness or give that full measure that makes for growth. For the Mind is the Builder, and ye build then through the application of same in thy dealings with the conditions, the circumstances, the relations with thy fellow man, either that which is eternal—as good, as righteousness, as patience, as brotherly love, as kindness—or ye starve thy soul with the husks that satisfy only the desires of the body for the moment.   1551-2

That we sow we must reap, and we must meet our own conditions as are created in our own minds, for the *Mind is* the *Builder*, and when we build a barrier between ourselves [and] our associates, our friends, our *families*, this we must, *of our own volition*, tear down . . . That of the spirit forces as are innate may become so subjugated by the desires of the flesh that they may become as nil, yet these are ever ready to be awakened and to exercise their prerogative in the life of each and every individual . . . [if] same . . . [is] allowed to manifest itself; but *self* must be subjugated . . . [for] such . . . [to] come about. In the *mind* . . . in the inner self . . . must the entity, the body, build . . . coming to the realization that the body *physical* has become so amenable, so low, as *not* to be able to control the appetite of a physical body—[Self] must submit itself to the will of another, that through same there may be created within the will, and there may be aroused within the spiritual forces, that element that may give life, light, health, strength, happiness to this body . . . do that.
                                                                4286-2

[This individual (4286) had become addicted to morphine and was being advised to undergo hypnosis in order to overcome this problem. The advice was followed and proved effective.]

Earthly sojourns or experiences bring those emotions that find their development in feeding upon same for the magnifying of their effect upon that as may be the mental or the soul self. For Mind being the Builder, ever, is both human and divine. And as the mind dwells, so does the application of that the teacher of teachers gave become effective; not by merely taking the thought may one whit be added but by *applying* in the material experience the law and the love of same—this makes for growth! For life and truth and understanding, and happiness—in its greater sense, are but a growth. For ye *grow* in grace, in knowledge, in understanding. And knowledge without wisdom is indeed a dangerous thing!   1301-1

Circumstances alter conditions in a material plane, but the spiritual and mental growth may not be altered [by circumstances]. For, only self may keep the entity from fulfilling those purposes for which it entered the material experience in the present.   2612-1

Just as has so oft been indicated, one doesn't fall out of a tree into heaven . . . or fly into heaven, but one grows in grace, in knowledge, in understanding, in perfecting within self those applications of tenets and truths that bring to the activities . . . spiritual . . . [and] mental growth. Then, the physical results are in keeping with the purposes. For it is in Him, the Giver, that we live and move and have our being. Individuals realize, or must realize, there is little they may do . . . [except] help others to help themselves. In so doing they add to their own stature in spirit, in mind . . . [and] body-purposes.   2746-2

In giving that which may be helpful at this time, consider that which is necessary for . . . soul development. While the mind, as it is commonly spoken of, is the builder, it—as the personality and individuality of an entity—has two phases. The mind functions irrespective of the body. Hence that which is builded for the development of the soul body is for expression of the soul mind, or superconscious mind . . . [The] mental mind . . . may be trained in a physical body to care for same. Hence . . . [the] more that the mind in its activity is of the soul's development, the less and less of self is expressed and more and more [there is expressed] the consciousness, the awareness, of a condition, an event, a feeling, an emotion . . . that deals with the attributes of the soul–body . . . [In this manner] the soul becomes aware of the presence of the creative conscience, the oneness of self in that which is the essence of life itself. When there is less and less of the personal desires, more and more does *patience* become a portion of the whole being—and . . . [there is] awareness of the soul's longings, the soul's desires, the soul's expressions of Him in *true*, pure love.   696-3

19

Miscellaneous Advice on the Mind

(Q) . . . **GIVE** me suggestions as to how to improve my work in school, and my memory . . .

(A) That which ye would attain . . . mull . . . as it were in thy mind, in thy consciousness. Then lay it aside, and meditate rather upon its application in every way and manner. Do this especially just before ye would rest in physical consciousness . . . or in sleep. And ye will find thy memory, thy ability to analyze . . . will [improve] . . .   1581-2

(Q) Will it be necessary for this soul-entity to return again in what we call the earth's plane?

(A) Dependent upon the application of self, self's abilities, in the development of the soul or subconscious mind.   220-1

Do not let thy reason overshadow or be in the way of love. For love thinketh no evil; it is not puffed up, it is kind, it is gentle, it is patient And Mind being the Builder, do not stand too oft upon thy privileges but rather humble thyself that ye may serve the more, that ye may bring to the consciousness of others that love that is so near at hand, and that only those who have turned their face the other way do not see or comprehend.   1404-1

Let that Mind be the Builder that is the intuitive force for the Christlike hope of man.   2655-1

In the beginning God created the heavens and the earth. How? The *Mind* of God *moved*, and matter, form, came into being. Mind, then, in God, the Father, is the Builder. How much more, then . . . should Mind be the builder in the experience of those that have put on Christ . . . For as He has given, "Let that mind be in you which was in the Christ, who thought it not robbery to make Himself equal with God" . . . That ye think, that ye put your Mind to work upon, to live upon, to feed upon, to live with, to abide with, to associate with in the mind, *that* your soul-body becomes!   262-78

. . . as relative to Creative Forces . . . these are set as rules: Law, God, Love, Creative Force—whatever term we may express same in—"What ye sow, ye reap." The Mind is the Builder. God *is*. Man is. And the mind is a portion of both the soul and the spirit, the directing force, and is also of the earth-earthy. Hence the injunction that has been given, "Be ye of one mind, one purpose, in Christ."   1265-3

Appendix A

From Reading 1947-3

MIND is the Builder: it is both spiritual and physical, and thus has its aspirations, its limitations, its fears, its hopes, its desires.

To determine . . . whether the emotions or influences which arise from one experience to another are from purely a mental aspiration of a physical desire, or from a spiritual aspect and hope in its relationships to the things desired of self, comparisons need to be drawn for the entity as to how, and in what manner judgments or choices are to be made.

The [entity] finds itself Body, Mind, Soul; just as seen in that after which it is patterned—Father, Son, Holy Spirit.

In the choices, then, it is seen that each of these phases of spiritual experience finds its own place of activity, as illustrated in the entity's experience in materiality.

The *Spirit* moved—or soul moved—and there was Light (Mind). The Light became the light of men—Mind [was] made aware of conscious existence in spiritual aspects or relationships as one to another.

The mind of the entity becomes aware of longings, innate in the inner self; also the arousing of emotions in the physical attributes of the body—just as indicated as to how these came into *being;* as self is a part of Creative Forces or God, Spirit, the Son. These are one. The body, mind and soul are one. Their desires must be one, their purposes, their aims must be one—then—to be ideal.

What, then, has this to do with the entity in its seeking for the use of its own abilities in the psychic, the mental, the material atmosphere in which it finds itself in the present?

There are laws, then [that] govern the physical, the mental, the spiritual body, and the attributes of each of these. The abuse of a physical law brings dis-ease and then disturbance to the physical organism, through which mental and spiritual portions of the body operate.

There are also promises, warnings, and governing forces, as has been indicated, for the physical and the mental and the spiritual being—as given by those forces and influences which manifest in the material world as respecting each of these.

As the Mind indicated, "I and the Father are one; he that abideth in me as I abide in the Father *hath eternal life.*" Not *will* have, not *may* have, but *hath*—now—is in eternal consciousness of being at a onement with eternal influence and force!

. . . this is the moving of the spirit that has brought . . . life [and] light, to the consciousness of the entity . . .

. . . If God had not given free will to man . . . would [men] have been able to be equal with Him? [A very good question to think about.]

Appendix B

From Readings 5754-1, 5754-2, and 5754-3

READING 5754-1: This psychic reading given by Edgar Cayce at his home on Arctic Crescent, Virginia Beach, Va., this fourteenth day of July, 1932, in accordance with request made by Hugh Lynn Cayce and those present: Edgar Cayce; Gertrude Cayce, conductor; Gladys Davis, stenographer; Mildred Davis; Edgar Evans Cayce. Time of reading 4:30 p.m.

G.C.: You will please outline clearly and comprehensively the material which should be presented to the general public in explaining just what occurs in the conscious, subconscious and spiritual forces of an entity while in the state known as sleep. Please answer the questions which will be asked regarding this:

E.C.: Yes. While there has been a great deal written and spoken regarding experiences of individuals in that state called sleep, there has only recently been the attempt to control or form any definite idea of what produces conditions in the unconscious, subconscious, or subliminal or subnormal mind, by attempts to produce a character—or to determine that which produces the character—of dream as had by an individual or entity. Such experiments may determine, for some minds, questions respecting the claim of some psychiatrist or psychoanalyst and through such experiments refute or determine the value of such in the study of certain character of mental disturbances in individuals; yet little of this may be called true analysis of what happens to the body, either physical, mental, subconscious or spiritual, when it loses itself in such repose. To be sure, there are certain definite conditions that take place respecting the physical, the conscious, and the subconscious, as well as spiritual forces of a body.

So, in analyzing such a state for a comprehensive understanding, all things pertaining to these various factors must be considered.

First, we would say, sleep is a shadow of, that intermission in earth's experiences of, that state called death; for the physical consciousness becomes unaware of existent conditions, save as are determined by the attributes of the physical that partake of the attributes of the imaginative or the subconscious and unconscious forces of that same body; that is, in a normal sleep (physical standpoint we are reasoning now) the *senses* are on guard, as it were, so that the auditory forces are those that are the more sensitive. The auditory sense being of the attributes or senses that are more universal in aspect, when matter in its evolution has become aware of itself being capable of taking from that about itself to sustain itself in its present state. That is as of the lowest to the highest of animate objects or beings. From the lowest of evolution to the highest, or to man.

So, then, we find that there are left what is ordinarily known as four other attributes that are acting independently and coordinatingly in *awareness* for a physical body to be conscious. These, in the state of sleep or repose, or rest, or exhaustion, or induced by any influence from the outside, have become *unaware* of that which is taking place about the object so resting.

Then, there is the effect that is had upon the body as to what becomes, then, more aware to those attributes of the body that are not aware of that existent about them, or it. The organs that are of that portion known as the inactive, or not necessary for conscious movement, keep right on with their functioning; yet there are periods during such a rest when even the heart, the circulation, may be said to be at rest. What, then, *is* that that is not in action during such period? That known as the sense of perception as related to the physical brain. Hence it may be truly said, by the authority of that given, that the auditory sense is sub-divided, and there is the act of hearing by feeling, the act of hearing by the sense of smell, the act of hearing by *all* the senses that are independent of the brain centers themselves, but are rather of the lymph centers—or throughout the entire sympathetic system is in such an accord as to be *more* aware, *more* acute, even though the body physical and brain-physical *is* at repose, or *unaware*.

Of what, then, does this sixth sense partake, that has to do so much with the entity's activities by those actions that may be brought about by that passing within the sense *range* of an entity when in repose, that may be called—in their various considerations or phases—experiences of *something* within that entity, as a dream—that may be either in toto to that which is to happen, is happening, or may be only presented in some form that is emblematical—to the body or those that would interpret such.

These, then—or this, then—the sixth sense, as it may be termed for consideration here, partakes of the *accompanying* entity that is ever on guard before the throne of the Creator itself, and is that that may be trained or submerged, or left to its *own* initiative until it makes either war *with* the self in some manner of expression—which must show itself in a material world as in dis-ease, or disease, or temper, or that we call the blues, or the grouches, or any form that may receive either in the waking state or in the sleep state, that has *enabled* the brain in its activity to become so changed or altered as to respond much in the manner as does a string tuned that vibrates to certain sound in the manner in which it is strung or played upon.

Then we find, this sense that governs such is that as may be known as the other self of the entity, or individual. Hence we find there must be some definite line that may be taken by that other self, and much that then has been . . . recorded—as to that which may produce certain given effects in the minds or bodies (not the minds, to be sure, for its active forces are upon that outside of that in which the mind, as ordinarily known, or the brain centers themselves, functions), but—as may be seen by all such experimentation, these may be produced—the same effect—upon the same individual, but they do not produce the same effect upon a different individual in the same environment or under the same circumstances. Then, this should lead one to know, to understand, that there is a *definite* connection between that we have chosen to term he sixth sense, or acting through the auditory forces of the body-physical, and the other self within self.

In purely physical, we find in sleep the body is *relaxed*—and there is little or no tautness within same, and those activities that function through the organs that are under the supervision of the subconscious or unconscious self, through the involuntary activities of an organism that has been set in motion by that impulse it has received from its first germ cell force, and its activity by the union *of* those forces that have been impelled or acted upon by that it has fed upon in all its efforts and activities that come, then it may be seen that these may be shown by due consideration—that the same body fed upon *meats,* and for a period—then the same body fed upon only herbs and fruits would *not* have the same character or activity of the other self in its relationship to that as would be experienced by the other self in its activity through that called the dream self.

We are through for the moment—present.

Reading 5754-2: Given the next day, July 15, 1932, at 11:30 a.m.

E.C.: Now, with that as has just been given, that there is an active force within each individual that functions in the manner of a sense when the body-physical is in sleep, repose or rest, we would then outline as to what are the functions of this we have chosen to call a sixth sense.

What relation does it bear with the normal physical recognized five senses of a physical-aware body? If these are active, what relation do they bear to this sixth sense?

Many words have been used in attempting to describe what the spiritual entity of a body is, and what relations this spirit or soul bears with or to the active forces within a physical normal body. Some have chosen to call this the cosmic body, and the cosmic body as a sense in the universal consciousness, or that portion of same that is a part of, or that body with which the individual, or man, is clothed in his advent into the material plane.

These are correct in many respects, yet by their very classification, or by calling them by names to designate their faculties or functionings, have been limited in many respects.

But what relation has this sixth sense (as has been termed in this presented) with this *soul* body, this cosmic consciousness? What relation has it with the faculties and functionings of the normal physical mind? Which must be trained? The sixth sense? or must the body be trained in its other functionings to the dictates of the sixth sense?

In that as presented, we find this has been termed, that this ability or this functioning that is so active when physical consciousness is laid aside—or, as has been termed by some poet, when the body rests in the arms of Morpheus—is nearer possibly to that as may be understandable by or to many; for, as given, this activity—as is seen—of a mind, or an attribute of the mind in physical activity—*leaves* a *definite* impression.

Upon what? The mental activities of the body, or upon the subconscious portion of the body (which, it has been termed that, it never forgets), upon the spiritual essence of the body, or upon the soul itself? These are questions, not statements! [At this point, some of you may be thinking, "But Edgar, we are here for answers rather than more questions!!]

In understanding, then, let's present illustrations as a pattern, that there may be comprehension of that which is being presented:

The activity, or this sixth sense activity, is the activating power or force of the other self. What other self? That which has been builded by the entity or body, or soul, through its experiences as a whole in the material and cosmic world or is as a faculty of the soul–body itself. Hence, as the illustration given, does the subconscious make aware to this active force when the body is at rest, or this sixth sense, some action on the part of self or another that is in disagreement with that which has been builded by that other self, then *this* is the warring of conditions or emotions within an individual. Hence we may find that an individual may from sorrow *sleep* and wake with a feeling of elation. What has taken place? We possibly may then understand what we are speaking of. There has been, and ever when the physical consciousness is at rest, the other self communes with the *soul* of the body . . . or it goes *out* into that realm of experience in the relationships of all experiences of that entity that may have been throughout the *eons* of time, or in correlating *with* that as it, that entity, *has* accepted as its criterion or standard of judgments, or justice within its sphere of activity.

Hence through such an association in sleep there may have come that peace, that understanding, that is accorded by that which has been correlated through that passage of the selves of a body in sleep. Hence we find the more spiritual–minded individuals are the more easily pacified, at peace, harmony, in normal active state as well as in sleep. Why? They have set before themselves (Now we are speaking of one individual!) that that *is* a criterion that may be wholly relied upon, for that from which an entity or soul sprang is its *concept*, its awareness of, the divine or creative forces within their experience. Hence they that have named the Name of the Son have put their trust in Him. He [is] their standard, their model, their hope, their activity. Hence we see how that the action through such sleep, or such quieting as to enter the silence— What do we mean by entering the silence? Entering the presence of that which *is* the criterion of the selves of an entity!

On the other hand oft we find one may retire with a feeling of elation, or peace, and awaken with a feeling of depression, of aloofness, of being alone, of being without hope, or of fear entering, and the *body-physical* awakes with that depression that makes itself as of low spirits, as is termed, or of coldness, gooseflesh over the body, in expressions of the forces. What has taken place? A comparison in that "arms of Morpheus," in that silence, in that relationship of the physical self being unawares of those comparisons between the soul and its experiences of that period with the experiences of itself throughout the ages, and the experiences may not have been remembered as a dream—but it lives *on*—and on, and must find its expression in the relationships of all it has experienced in whatever sphere of activity it may have found itself. Hence we find oft individual circumstances of where a spiritual-minded individual in the material plane (that is, to outward appearances of individuals so viewing same) suffering oft under pain, sickness, sorrow, and the like. What takes place? The experiences of the soul are meeting that which it has merited, for the clarification for the associations of itself with that whatever has been set as its ideal. If one has set self in array against that of love as manifested by the Creator, in its activity brought into material plane, then there *must* be a continual—continual—*warring* of those elements. By the comparison we may find, then, how it was, that energy of creation manifested in the Son—by the activities of the Son in the material plane, could say, "He sleeps," while to the outward eye it was death; for *He was*—and *is*—and ever will be Life and Death in one; for as we find ourselves *in* His presence, that we have built in the soul makes for that condemnation or that pleasing of the presence of that in His presence. So, my son, let thine lights be in Him, for these are the *manners* through which all may come to an understanding of the activities; for, as was given, "I was in the Spirit on the Lord's day." "I was caught up to the seventh heaven. Whether I was in the body or out of the body I cannot tell." What was taking place? The subjugation of the physical attributes in accord and attune with its infinite force as set as its ideal brought to that soul, "Well done, thou good and faithful servant, enter into the joys of thy Lord." "He that would be the greatest among you—" Not as the Gentiles, not as the heathen, not as the scribes or Pharisees, but "He that would be the greatest will be the *servant* of all."

What, then, has this to do—you ask—with the subject of sleep? Sleep—that period when the soul takes stock of that it has acted upon during one rest period to another, making or drawing—as it were—the comparisons that make for Life itself in its *essence*, as for harmony, peace, kindness—these are the fruits of the spirit. Hate, harsh words, unkind thoughts, oppressions and the like, these are the fruits of the evil forces, or Satan and the soul either abhors that it has passed, or enters into the joy of its Lord. Hence we see the activities of same. This [is] an *essence* of that which is intuitive in the active forces. Why should this be so in one portion, or one part of a body, rather than another? How received woman her awareness? Through the sleep of a man! Hence *intuition* is an attribute of that made aware through the suppression of those forces from that from which it sprang, yet endowed *with* all of those abilities and forces of its Maker that make for same its activity in an *aware* world, or—if we choose to term it such—a three-dimensional world, a *material* world, where its beings must see a materialization to become aware of its existence in that plane; yet all are aware that the essence of Life itself, as the air that is breathed—carries those elements that are not aware consciously of any existence to the body, yet the body subsists, lives upon such. In sleep all things become possible, as one finds self flying through space, lifting, or being chased, or what not, by those very things that make for a comparison of that which has been builded by the very soul of the body itself.

What, then, is the sixth sense? Not the soul, not the conscious mind, not the subconscious mind, not intuition alone, not any of those cosmic forces—but the very force or activity of the soul in its experience through *whatever* has been the experience of that soul itself. The same as we would say, is the mind of the body, the body? No! Is the sixth sense, then, the soul? No! No more than the mind is the body! For the soul is the *body* of, or the spiritual essence of, an entity manifested in this material plane.

We are through for the present.

Reading 5754-3: Given later that day at 4:45 p.m. on July 15, 1932.

E.C.: Yes, we have that which has been given here. Now, as we have that condition that exists with the body and this functioning, or this sense, or this ability of sleep and sense, or a sixth sense, just what, how, may this knowledge be used to advantage for an individual's development towards that it would attain?

As to how it may be used, then, depends upon what is the ideal of that individual; for, as has been so well pointed out in Holy Writ, if the ideal of the individual is lost, then the abilities for that facility or that sense of an individual to contact the spiritual forces are gradually lost, or barriers are builded that prevent this from being a sensing of the nearness of an individual to a spiritual development.

As to those who are nearer the spiritual realm, their visions, dreams, and the like, are more often—and are more often retained by the individual; for, as is seen as a first law, it is self-preservation. Then self rarely desires to condemn self, save when the selves are warring one with another, as are the elements within a body when eating of that which produces what is termed a nightmare—they are warring with the senses of the body, and partake either of those things that make afraid, or produce visions of the nature as partaking of the elements that are taken within the system, and active within same itself. These may be given as examples of what it is all about.

Then, how may this be used to develop a body in its relationship to the material, the mental, and the spiritual forces?

Whether the body desires or not, in sleep the consciousness physically is laid aside. As to what will be that it will seek, depends upon what has been builded as that it would associate itself with, physically, mentally, spiritually, and the closer the association in the mental mind in the physical elements, then—as has been seen by even those attempting to produce a certain character of vision or dream—these follow much in that; for another law that is universal becomes active! Like begets like! That which is sown in honor is reaped in glory. That which is sown in corruption cannot be reaped in glory; and the likings are associations that are the companions of that which has been builded; for such experiences as dreams, visions and the like, are but the *activities* in the unseen world of the real self of an entity.

Ready for questions.

(Q) How may one train the sixth sense?
(A) This has just been given; that which is constantly associated in the mental visioning in the imaginative forces, that which is constantly associated with the senses of the body, that will it develop toward. What is that which is and may be sought? When under stress *many* an individual—There are *no* individuals who haven't at *some time* been warned as respecting that that may arise in their daily or physical existence! Have they heeded? Do they heed to that as may be given as advice? No! It must be experienced!

(Q) How may one be constantly guided by the accompanying entity on guard at the Throne?
(A) It is there! It's as to whether they desire [guidance] or not! It doesn't leave but is the active force! As to its ability to *sense* the variations in the experiences that are seen, is, as has been given in the illustration—"As to whether in the body or out of the body, I cannot tell." Hence this sense is that ability of the entity to associate its physical, mental or spiritual self to that realm that it, the entity, or the mind of the soul, seek for its association during such periods . . . This might confuse some, for—as has been given—the subconscious and the abnormal, or the unconscious conscious, is the mind of the soul; that is, the sense that this is

used, as being that subconscious or subliminal self that is on guard ever with the Throne itself; for, has it not been said, "He has given his angels charge concerning thee, lest at any time thou dashest thy foot against a stone?" Have you heeded? Then He is near. Have you disregarded? He has withdrawn to thine own self . . . That self that has been builded, that that is as the companion, that must be presented—that is presented—is before the Throne itself! *Consciousness* [physical] consciousness . . . Man seeks this for his *own* diversion. In the sleep [the soul] seeks the *real* diversion, or the *real* activity of self.

(Q) What governs the experiences of the astral body while in the fourth-dimensional plane during sleep?
(A) This is, as has been given, that upon which it has been fed. That which it has builded; that which it seeks; that which the mental mind, the subconscious mind, the subliminal mind, *seeks!* That governs. Then we come to an understanding of that, "He that would find must seek." In the physical or material this we understand. That is [also] a pattern of the subliminal or the spiritual self.

(Q) What state or trend of development is indicated if an individual does not remember dreams?
(A) [This indicates] The negligence of its associations, both physical, mental and spiritual. [This] Indicates a very negligible personage!

(Q) Does one dream continually but simply fail to remember consciously?
(A) Continues an association or withdraws from that which *is* its right, or its ability to associate! There is no difference in the unseen world to that that is visible, save in the unseen so much greater expanse or space may be covered! Does one always desire to associate itself with others? Do individuals always seek companionship in this or that period of their experiences in each day? Do they withdraw themselves from [contact]? That desire lies or carries on! . . . It's a *natural* experience! It's *not* an unnatural [experience]. Don't seek for unnatural or supernatural [experiences]! It is the natural—it is nature—it is God's activity! His association with man. [It is] His *desire* to make for man a way for an

understanding! Is there seen or understood fully that illustration that was given of the Son of Man, that while those in the ship were afraid because of the elements the Master of the sea, of the elements, slept? What associations may there have been with that sleep? Was it a natural withdrawing? Yet when spoken to, the sea and the winds obeyed His voice. Thou may do even as He; wilt thou make thyself aware whether [it is] that awareness through the ability of those forces within self to communicate with, [and] understand those elements of the spiritual life *in* the conscious and unconscious—these be one.

(Q) Is it possible for a conscious mind to dream while the astral or spirit body is absent?

(A) There may be [such] dreams—(This is a division here)—A conscious mind, while the body is absent, is as one's ability to divide self and do two things at once, as is seen by the activities of the mental mind. The ability to read music and play is using different faculties of the same mind. Different portions of the same consciousness. Then, for one faculty to function while another is functioning in a different direction is not only possible but probable, dependent upon the ability of the individual to concentrate, or to centralize their various places, those functionings that are manifest of the spiritual forces in the material plane. *Beautiful*, isn't it?

(Q) What connection is there between the physical or conscious mind and the spiritual body during sleep or during an astral experience?

(A) It's as has been given, that *sensing*! With what? That separate sense, or the ability of sleep, that makes for acuteness with those forces in the physical being that are manifest in everything animate. As the unfolding of the rose, the quickening in the womb, of the grain as it buds forth, the awakening in all nature of that which has been set by the divine forces, to make the awareness of its presence in *matter*, or material things.

We are through for the present.

A.R.E. PRESS

The A.R.E. Press publishes books, videos, and audiotapes meant to improve the quality of our readers' lives—personally, professionally, and spiritually. We hope our products support your endeavors to realize your career potential, to enhance your relationships, to improve your health, and to encourage you to make the changes necessary to live a loving, joyful, and fulfilling life.

For more information or to receive a free catalog, call:

1–800–723–1112

Or write:

A.R.E. Press
215 67th Street
Virginia Beach, VA 23451-2061

DISCOVER HOW THE EDGAR CAYCE MATERIAL CAN HELP YOU!

The Association for Research and Enlightenment, Inc. (A.R.E.®), was founded in 1931 by Edgar Cayce. Its international headquarters are in Virginia Beach, Virginia, where thousands of visitors come year-round. Many more are helped and inspired by A.R.E.'s local activities in their own hometowns or by contact via mail (and now the Internet!) with A.R.E. headquarters.

People from all walks of life, all around the world, have discovered meaningful and life-transforming insights in the A.R.E. programs and materials, which focus on such areas as personal spirituality, holistic health, dreams, family life, finding your best vocation, reincarnation, ESP, meditation, and soul growth in small-group settings. Call us today at our toll-free number:

1-800-333-4499

or

Explore our electronic visitors center on the
Internet: **http://www.edgarcayce.org.**

We'll be happy to tell you more about how the work of the A.R.E. can help you!

A.R.E.
215 67th Street
Virginia Beach, VA 23451-2061